Professor M. D. KAMMARI

The Development
by J. V. STALIN
of the
Marxist-Leninist Theory
of the
National Question

★

FOREIGN LANGUAGES PUBLISHING HOUSE
Moscow 1951

PUBLISHER'S NOTE

This pamphlet is a translation of an article in the symposium *To Joseph Vissarionovich Stalin—From the Academy of Sciences of the U.S.S.R.* published at the end of 1949 in commemoration of J. V. Stalin's seventieth birthday by the Publishing House of the Academy of Sciences of the U.S.S.R., Moscow.

CONTENTS

                                                          Page

1. SUBSTANTIATION OF THE BOLSHEVIK PARTY'S PROGRAM ON THE NATIONAL QUESTION 8

2. THE CREATION OF THE U.S.S.R.—THE GREAT COMMONWEALTH OF SOCIALIST NATIONS 33

Joseph Vissarionovich Stalin, the genius who is continuing the great cause of Lenin, has developed the theory of Marxism-Leninism applicably to the new epoch in history which is rightly called the Stalin epoch. This is the epoch of proletarian revolutions and of the proletarian dictatorship, the epoch of the building of Communism in the U.S.S.R., the Soviet epoch in the history of society. Applicably to this Soviet epoch, J. V. Stalin also developed the Marxist-Leninist theory of the national question.

Defining Lenin's new contribution to the solution of the national and colonial question, J. V. Stalin stated that Lenin proceeded from the basic initial ideas advanced by Marx and Engels in analyzing the events in Ireland, India, China, the Central European countries, Poland and Hungary in the period of premonopolist capitalism. Lenin and Stalin based themselves on these ideas and developed them applicably to the epoch of imperialism and proletarian revolution.

"Lenin's new contribution in this field," said Comrade Stalin, "was:

"a) he gathered these ideas into one harmonious system of views on national and colonial revolutions in the epoch of imperialism;

"b) he connected the national and colonial question with the overthrow of imperialism;

"c) he declared the national and colonial question to be a component part of the general question of the international proletarian revolution."*

In close collaboration with V. I. Lenin, Comrade Stalin elaborated these questions of the theory and tactics of the socialist revolution and of the proletarian dictatorship. Comrade Stalin created the Marxist theory of the nation, worked out from all aspects the Party's program and policy on the national question, developed the ideas of Leninism applicably to the *Soviet* period, and further elaborated the national question in connection with the tasks of the proletarian dictatorship and of the building of communist society. J. V. Stalin elaborated from all aspects the ques-

---

* The above excerpt is from " Interview With the First American Trade Union Delegation" (see V. I. Lenin, *Selected Works,* Two-Vol. ed., Vol. 1, Part 1, Moscow 1950, p. 52).

tions concerning the building of a multinational socialist state, the abolition of national oppression and of the actual inequality of nations, the organization of collaboration between the new, Soviet, socialist nations on the basis of the Soviet system, on the basis of Socialism, and the development of the culture of the socialist nations, i. e., culture which is national in form and socialist in content. Comrade Stalin elaborated the question of the united front between the Soviet socialist nations and the international working-class movement for emancipation and with the liberation movements of the oppressed peoples of the dependent countries and colonies, regarding these latter movements as the heavy reserves of the socialist revolution. J. V. Stalin developed and raised to a new and higher stage the ideology of proletarian internationalism and friendship among the nations.

The works of J. V. Stalin provide a comprehensive, profound and scientific substantiation of the Bolshevik Party's program and policy on the national question and serve as a guide for all fraternal Communist Parties.

1

SUBSTANTIATION OF THE BOLSHEVIK PARTY'S PROGRAM ON THE NATIONAL QUESTION

Lenin and Stalin began to elaborate the national question at the very birth of the Bolshevik Party. This is understandable, because it was impossible to build a revolutionary proletarian party in a multinational state and to define its policy and tactics in the struggle for Socialism without a scientific, Marxist solution of the national question.

Lenin called tsarist Russia a "prison of the nations." Comrade Stalin says that Russia "was the home of every kind of oppression—capitalist, colonial and militarist—in its most inhuman and barbarous form."* Russia was a multinational country. For this reason the working-class movement in Russia was faced with exceptionally difficult and complicated tasks such

---

* J. Stalin, *Problems of Leninism*, Moscow 1947, p. 16.

as the proletariat in no other country in the world was faced with. The Russian proletariat had to find the proper approach to the multi-national peasantry among the oppressed nations in Russia.

From the very outset of his revolutionary activities J. V. Stalin exposed bourgeois nationalism and, in conjunction with Lenin, championed the principle of *proletarian internationalism* as the basis of Russian Social-Democracy, in opposition to the Bundists, Caucasian Federalists and nationalists who camouflaged themselves with socialist phraseology; he developed the idea of the *hegemony of the proletariat* in the national-liberation movement. J. V. Stalin developed these ideas in the course of the struggle against the nationalism of the majority in the Mesame-dasi group,* in the struggle against the nationalism preached by Noah Jordania. These ideas are also reflected in the leading article in the first issue of the newspaper *Brdzola*, 1901, entitled "Statement by the Editors," in a comprehensive program article entitled "The Russian Social-Democratic Party and Its Immediate Tasks" published in the same newspaper No. 2-3 (cf. *Collected Works*, Vol. 1), and in his subsequent works.

J. V. Stalin's work *How Social-Democrats*

---

* The first Social-Democratic organization in Georgia.

Understand the National Question (September, 1904) is a splendid commentary on the national program of the R.S.D.L.P. In it Comrade Stalin substantiates and develops the Party's theory and program of the national question and subjects to destructive criticism the opportunist principle of splitting up the proletariat according to nationality, the attempts of the opportunists and nationalists to divide the working class by means of national barriers. J. V. Stalin champions the consistently international type and principle of building the proletarian class organizations and emphasizes that the destruction of national barriers and the amalgamation of the workers irrespective of nationality in united proletarian organizations are decisive conditions for the victory of the working class. In this work, J. V. Stalin stands forth as a great theoretician on the national question, wielding the Marxist dialectical method with masterly skill. This work contains in the germ the ideas that he later developed in his work *Marxism and the National Question.*

Exposing the ideology of nationalism, J. V. Stalin brilliantly employs the Marxist dialectical method in solving the national question, creatively develops the idea of proletarian internationalism, substantiates and concretizes the principles of the Bolshevik program on the national question, i. e., the right of nations to self-determination, champions complete equality of rights for all citizens irrespective of sex, religion, race or nationality, and the rallying of all the workers in Russia irrespective of nationality around a *single* proletarian party and in united workers' organizations built up on the *international* principle.

Such was the starting point of the *proletarian* solution of the national question—a solution that ensured the *hegemony of the proletariat* in the national-liberation movement; such was the starting point of the *proletarian, international* way of liberating the oppressed nations elaborated by Lenin and Stalin.

In order utterly to expose nationalism and scientifically to substantiate the Party's program and policy on the national question it was necessary to elaborate the Marxist theory of the nation. This was done by J. V. Stalin in his work *Marxism and the National Question* (January 1913).

The bourgeois ideologists, and the reformists after them, look at a nation from the metaphysical and idealistic point of view; they regard a nation as something fixed once and for all; they reduce nation to a mystical "national spirit," to a "national character and will," to a "national soul" or to "racial blood and soul"; they try to deduce nation from "national consciousness and will" and not, on the contrary, to deduce a nation's consciousness and will from the conditions of its material existence.

J. V. Stalin exposed the anti-scientific and reactionary character of these theories and countered them with the scientific, Marxist theory of the nation.

A nation is not something eternal and immutable. Nation is a historical category: historically, nations arise for the first time in the epoch of rising capitalism, of the elimination of feudal disintegration. The development of capitalism, trade and the market, links up different regions with populations speaking the same language in a single economic whole.

Nation must not be confused with race and tribe; a national community must not be confused with a racial or tribal community, as the bourgeois sociologists do, because nations arise in the process of fusion of people of different races and tribes.

Scientifically generalizing the process of the rise and development of nations, J. V. Stalin has given the following classical, Marxist definition of a nation:

"*A nation is a historically evolved, stable community of people which arose on the basis of a common language, territory, economic life, and psychological make-up manifested in a common culture.*

"It goes without saying that a nation, like every other historical phenomenon, is subject to the law of change, has its history, its beginning and end."*

It is only when all these four attributes are present that we have a nation, Comrade Stalin explains; it is enough for even one of them to be absent for a nation to cease to be a nation.

This theory of a nation has received general recognition in the Bolshevik Party. In his work *The National Question and Leninism*, written in 1929 and first published in Vol. 11 of his *Collected Works*, Comrade Stalin criticizes attempts to "supplement" this definition of a nation with a fifth attribute, namely, the possession by a nation of its own, separate national state. According to the scheme of the authors of this "supplement," only such nations could be recognized as nations as have their own state separate from others, and all the oppressed nations which have no independent statehood would have to be deleted from the category of nations. Comrade Stalin showed that, in theory, this scheme leads to absurd conclusions, and in politics it leads to the justification of

---

* J. Stalin, *Marxism and the National and Colonial Question*, Moscow 1940, p. 7.

national imperialist oppression. This scheme was to the advantage of the bourgeois nationalists who opposed the amalgamation of the national Soviet Republics in a single Union State—the U.S.S.R.*

Having created a Marxist theory of the nation, J. V. Stalin criticized the bourgeois-nationalist theories of O. Bauer and K. Renner, the chief theoreticians of the Second International on the national question. Bauer and Renner defined a nation as a people possessing a "common culture," as "a union of similarly thinking and similarly speaking persons" not bound by a common territory and economic life. Bauer even went further and asserted that a common language is not an essential attribute of a nation. This theory divorced nation and national character from the historical soil, from the material basis on which a nation arises, lives and develops. Confusing nation with race, tribe or religious caste, this theory regards a nation as something immutable and eternal. As Comrade Stalin said, Bauer's "nation" differed in no way from the mystical "national spirit" of the spiritualists; it is not a living, really active nation, but something elusive, invisible and transcendental.

---

* J. Stalin, *The National Question and Leninism*, Moscow 1950, pp. 8, 9, 10.

From the rise of Leninism as Marxism of the epoch of imperialism and proletarian revolutions right up to the victory of the Great October Socialist Revolution, two theories and two programs on the national question contended against each other in the working-class movement: one was the Russian, Bolshevik, revolutionary Lenin-Stalin theory; the other was the reformist, Austrian Bauer-Renner theory, which was accepted by Kautsky, and following him, by the Trotskyites, the Bund and the other nationalist groups in Russia.

Basing themselves on their idealistic and metaphysical theory of the nation, Bauer and Renner included in their program the demand for the artificial creation of nations, for the amalgamation of people not bound by a common language, territory and economic life in separate national communities for the purpose of administering the respective nation's "cultural" affairs. On the basis of this theory the program of so-called "cultural-national autonomy" was built. Comrade Stalin showed that this program is both utopian and reactionary. Its aim is artificially to unite in a nation people whom the development of capitalism is constantly, daily, compelling to migrate from one country to another, in search of work for example. This program is reactionary because its aim is to shut the workers within the shell of their nation, to subject them to the ideology of bourgeois nationalism, to shatter international proletarian solidarity. This program actually did lead to the break-up of Austrian Social-Democracy, trade unions and other workers' organizations into separate national groups; it led to the collapse of the international unity of the working-class movement in Austria-Hungary, to national bickering, to the growth of nationalism and chauvinism. This was a *reformist* program; its aim was to solve the national question not on the basis of revolution, but on the basis of reform, of "slight amendments" of the Constitution of the Austro-Hungarian monarchy. It was a *nationalist* and *imperialist* program; it was based on the principle of the integrity of the Austro-Hungarian Empire, which oppressed other nations (the Slavs) and with this in view degraded the right of nations to self-determination to miserable and meagre "cultural-national autonomy." Pursuing the aim of preserving the state power and privileges of the dominant nation, it perpetuated the oppression of the Slavonic nations by the Germans.

Comrade Stalin countered the bourgeois-nationalist ideology, theory and program of the parties of the Second International with the thoroughly consistent, scientific, Marxist world-outlook, with the Marxist theory and method of solving the national question, with the proletarian international method of solving the national question, the only correct method.

As Comrade Stalin teaches us, the Marxist solution of the national question requires that strict account be taken of the economic, political and cultural environmental conditions in which nations live, and that these conditions be regarded from the angle of their process of *change and development*, i.e., in conformity with the requirements of Marxist dialectics. A solution which is correct for a nation in one period and under one set of conditions will be unsuitable in another period and under another set of conditions. A solution which is correct for one country and for one nation may prove to be unsuitable for another country and another nation.

"*The concrete historical conditions* as the starting point, *the dialectical presentation of the problem* as the only correct way of presenting it—such is the key to the solution of the national problem."* (My italics.—M.K.)

In conformity with this dialectical, Marxist presentation of the national question, J. V. Stalin linked its solution in our country in the period preceding the First World War with the tasks of

---

* J. Stalin, *Marxism and the National and Colonial Question,* Moscow 1940, p. 22.

the bourgeois-democratic revolution, and in the period of the First World War and the 1917 Revolution in Russia with the tasks of the *socialist* revolution.

J. V. Stalin pointed out that a condition for the solution of the national question is the radical democratic transformation of the state, i. e., *revolution*; but at the same time he emphasized that complete peace among the nations, i. e., the complete and actual solution of the national question is possible only under Socialism. He took as his starting point Lenin's theory that the bourgeois-democratic revolution must grow into the socialist revolution; he took into account the opening of the epoch of imperialism, of imperialist wars and the growth of national-liberation movements this inevitably brings in its train. "When in 1912 we Russian Marxists were drawing up the first draft of our national program," Comrade Stalin relates, "no serious movement for independence yet existed in any of the border regions of the Russian Empire. Nevertheless, we deemed it necessary to include in our program the point on the right of nations to self-determination, i. e., the right of every nationality to secede and exist as an independent state. Why? Because we based ourselves not only on what then existed, but also on what was developing and impending in the general system of international relations; that is, we took into account not only the present, but also the future."*

With the foresight of genius Comrade Stalin perceived this future and as early as 1913 pointed to the connection between the solution of the national question and the opening of the epoch of imperialism and imperialist wars and with the complications, crises and revolutions these would bring in their train. Noting that Russia is situated between Europe and Asia and that "the growth of democracy in Asia is inevitable," Comrade Stalin wrote: "The growth of imperialism in Europe is not fortuitous. In Europe, capital finds itself restricted, and it is striving towards foreign countries in search of new markets, cheap labour and new fields of investment. But this leads to external complications and to war.... It is quite possible, therefore, that a combination of internal and external factors may arise in which one or another nationality in Russia may find it necessary to raise and settle the question of its independence. And, of course, it is not for Marxists to create obstacles in such cases."** This thesis of Comrade Stalin's was subsequently fully con-

---

* J. Stalin, *Marxism and the National and Colonial Question*, Moscow 1940, p. 177.
** *Ibid.*, p. 49.

firmed during the war and after the war, in the period of the October Socialist Revolution.

Basing himself on the conditions of the new epoch, J. V. Stalin substantiated the Party's *program* slogan of *the right of nations to self-determination*, including the right to secede, and the need for *international solidarity of the workers* irrespective of nationality in united proletarian organizations as *most important points in the solution of the national question*.

J. V. Stalin exposed the nationalism of the theoreticians of the Second International (O. Bauer and K. Renner) which they had so cunningly camouflaged with socialist and internationalist phraseology. He pointed out that the principle of dividing the workers according to nationality that they advanced served to corrupt the workers by imbuing them with the ideology of bourgeois nationalism and cultivating national bigotry.

The principle advanced by the Bolsheviks that proletarian organizations must be built on an international basis was, on the contrary, *a tremendous lesson in proletarian internationalism*.

Proletarian internationalism cannot be reconciled with bourgeois nationalism. One or the other principle must triumph. There is no middle course: conflicting principles triumph over one another, they are not to be reconciled. In solving the national question J. V. Stalin consistently adhered to the principle of proletarian internationalism, the principle of Bolshevik partisanship. The theoretical principles of the Party's program on the national question elaborated by J. V. Stalin were a masterly generalization of the revolutionary experience and practice of the Bolshevik Party, of the practical activities the Bolsheviks conducted in Russia under the guidance of Lenin and Stalin.

How highly V. I. Lenin appraised the theoretical and practical political significance of this experience and its generalization by J. V. Stalin can be seen from the letter Lenin wrote to A. M. Gorky in February 1913, in which the experience in building the Party organization and in conducting Party activities on internationalist principles as was done in the Caucasus under Stalin's leadership is described as the *only correct proletarian* solution of the national question.*

On learning that some of the members of the editorial board of *Prosveshcheniye* proposed to consider Stalin's article as a subject for debate, Lenin emphatically opposed this: "Of course, we are absolutely opposed," he wrote. "The article is *very good*. This is a burning question, and we

---

* V. I. Lenin, *Collected Works,* 4th Russ. ed., Vol. 35, p. 58.

will not yield one iota of our principles to the Bundist riffraff."*

J. V. Stalin's work was a comprehensive substantiation of the Bolshevik Party's program on the national question and delivered a crushing blow at the theories of the Bundists, Liquidators, Mensheviks and Trotskyites who were poisoning the working-class movement with the venom of nationalism.

Lenin highly appraised this work of Stalin's and singled it out as the best in the whole of the theoretical Marxist literature on the national question. In his article "The National Program of the R.S.D.L.P." (December 1913) Lenin wrote:

"In theoretical Marxian literature ... the principles of the Social-Democratic national program, have already been dealt with recently (in this connection Stalin's article stands in the forefront)."**

Stalin's work *Marxism and the National Question* was the most important Bolshevik pronouncement on the national question in the prewar international arena. It was the Bolshevik theory of and program declaration on the national question.

"Two methods, two programs, two outlooks on

---

* V. I. Lenin, *Collected Works*, 4th Russ. ed., Vol 19, p. 535, Note 130.
** *Ibid.*, p. 488.

the national question were sharply contrasted in this work—that of the Second International and that of Leninism. Stalin worked with Lenin to demolish the opportunist views and dogmas of the Second International on this question.... Stalin, in this work, presents a Marxist theory of nations, formulates the priciples of the Bolshevik solution of the national problem (which demands that it be treated as part of the general problem of the revolution and inseparably from the entire international situation in the era of imperialism), and gives the theoretical foundation of the Bolshevik principle of international working-class solidarity."*

Defending the Bolshevik program and policy on the national question against the attacks of the Trotskyites at the Seventh (April) Conference of the R.S.D.L.P. (Bolsheviks) in 1917, J. V. Stalin said:

"Insofar as it is steering a course for the socialist revolution, Social-Democracy must support the revolutionary movement of the nations against imperialism.

"Either we deem it necessary to create a rear for the vanguard of the socialist revolution in the shape of the peoples who are rising against national oppression—in which case we are laying a

---

* *J. Stalin, A Short Biography,* Moscow 1951, pp. 45-46.

bridge between the West and the East—in which case we are really steering a course for the world socialist revolution; or we do not do so—in which case we will find ourselves isolated, in which case we renounce the tactics of utilizing for the purpose of destroying imperialism all revolutionary movements among the oppressed nationalities."*

This is a remarkably clear and profound substantiation of the new, Leninist-Stalinist presentation of the national question in connection with the course that was taken for the socialist revolution.

When organizing the victory of the Great October Revolution, Lenin and Stalin taught the Party to direct the stream of the national-liberation movement of the oppressed peoples into the channel of the socialist revolution. "The triumph of the revolution—such is the only path of liberation of the peoples of Russia from national oppression. . . .

"Either the peoples of Russia support the workers' revolutionary struggle for power—in which case they will achieve emancipation, or they do not support it—in which case they will no more see emancipation than they will see their own ears."**

This is how Comrade Stalin presented the question in all its acuteness on the eve of the Octo-

---

* J. V. Stalin, *Collected Works,* Russ. ed., Vol. 3, p. 56.
** *Ibid.,* p. 209.

ber Revolution, exposing the bourgeois counterrevolution, its policy of national oppression, the very policy that threatened the "dissolution" of Russia which the bourgeois press hypocritically accused the Bolsheviks of causing. The Bolshevik Party pursued the line of the voluntary amalgamation of the nations on the basis of free self-determination, complete equality of rights and mutual confidence and friendship among the nations, for only such an amalgamation could be real and durable.

In his article "The October Revolution and the National Question,"* J. V. Stalin showed concretely how the fundamental contradictions of capitalism on the national question are solved in the process of growth of the bourgeois-democratic revolution into the proletarian revolution and with the establishment of the proletarian dictatorship, and how, in this connection, the character and significance of national movements undergo a radical change: the bourgeois-national movement passes into the camp of imperialist reaction; the socialist movement of the workers and peasants of the oppressed nationalities triumphs on the basis of the struggle to establish the power of the Soviets.

---

* *Ibid.*, Vol. 4.

Generalizing the experience of the first year of the proletarian dictatorship, J. V. Stalin said: "the national question is entirely determined by the conditions of the social environment, by the character of the ruling power in the country and, in general, by the whole course of social development."*

The bourgeois conception of self-determination of nations was exposed in the course of the revolution. The socialist conception of the principle of self-determination of nations triumphed; the Party's Lenin-Stalin slogan: "all power to the toiling masses of the oppressed nationalities" but not to the national bourgeoisie, triumphed. Sweeping aside the chauvinist and cosmopolitan theories of the Trotskyites who asserted that the socialist revolution "annuls" the principles of self-determination of nations and defence of the fatherland, J. V. Stalin emphasized: "Actually, not the principles of self-determination and 'defence of the fatherland,' but their bourgeois interpretation is annulled."**

Developing further the *new* contribution that Leninism made to the treasury of Marxism on the national question, J. V. Stalin emphasized that the presentation and solution of the national ques-

---

* J. V. Stalin, *Collected Works*, Russ. ed., Vol. 4, p. 155.
** *Ibid.*, p. 166.

tion in Leninism differs radically from the way this question was presented and solved in the period of the Second International.

Comrade Stalin points to four fundamental points that distinguish the *new* presentation of the national question in Leninism:

The *first point* is that the national question, as a part, has been merged with the general question of the emancipation of the colonies, as a whole....

The *second point* is that the vague slogan of the right of nations to self-determination has been replaced by the clear revolutionary slogan of the right of nations and colonies to political secession and the formation of independent states....

The *third point* is the disclosure of the organic connection between the national and colonial question and the question of the power of capital, of the overthrow of capitalism, of the dictatorship of the proletariat....

The *fourth point* is that a new element has been introduced into the national question—the element of real (and not merely juridical) equalization of nations (helping and encouraging the backward nations to raise themselves to the cultural and economic level of the more advanced nations), as one of the conditions necessary for securing fraternal cooperation between the toiling masses of the various nations (cf. "The National

Question Presented"*). This presentation of the national question, given in 1921, J. V. Stalin developed also in his subsequent works, particularly in his lectures *The Foundations of Leninism* (April 1924).

The parties affiliated to the Second International looked at the national question from the *reformist* angle as a separate, independent question having no connection with the question of overthrowing imperialism, of the proletarian revolution, i.e., they looked at it from the metaphysical, idealistic, *bourgeois* angle. Leninism, in complete conformity with the requirements of the dialectical method, examines the national question in connection with the proletarian class struggle, the proletarian revolution, and the proletarian dictatorship.

From the very outset the leaders of the Second International carefully evaded (and now evade) the question of the liberation of the peoples of the dependent countries and colonies from imperialist oppression. They usually confined the national question to a narrow range of questions that chiefly concerned the so-called "civilized" nations. They did not dare to put white and coloured, "civilized" and "uncivilized" peoples on a par and

---
* J. Stalin, *Marxism and the National and Colonial Question*, Moscow 1940, pp. 98, 99, 100, 101.

thus tacitly agreed with the racial ideology and policy of imperialism. The leaders of the Second International (O. Bauer, K. Renner, K. Kautsky and others) slipped into the *bourgeois* interpretation of the right of nations to self-determination. They converted the idea of self-determination from a weapon in the struggle against annexations into an instrument for justifying annexations. Leninism exposed this deception by *widening* the conception of self-determination and interpreting it as the right of the oppressed peoples of dependent countries and colonies to complete secession, as the right of nations to independent state existence. The idea of self-determination was thus transformed from an instrument for deceiving the masses "into an instrument for exposing all and sundry imperialist aspirations and chauvinist machinations, into an instrument for the political education of the masses in the spirit of internationalism."*

The parties affiliated to the Second International were content with declarations about "equal rights for nations," and "equality of nations," and obscured the fact that under imperialism, when one group of nations (the minority) lives by exploiting another group of nations (the majority),

---

* J. Stalin, *Problems of Leninism*, Moscow 1947, p. 60.

"equality of nations" is just a hypocritical phrase, a mockery of the oppressed and exploited nations. Leninism exposed these mendacious declarations and stated that declarations about "equality of nations" that are not backed by direct support of the struggle for liberation waged by the oppressed nations are empty and false.

Revealing the extremely profound contradictions of imperialism and showing that the bankruptcy of its policy on the national-colonial question is inevitable, J. V. Stalin proved that the tendency to create national states and the tendency towards the amalgamation of nations are *irreconcilable* under imperialism, because the latter cannot exist without exploiting colonies and forcibly keeping them within the framework of an "integral whole," because imperialism can "unite" nations only by annexations and colonial conquests, which inevitably leads to a struggle of the oppressed nations against the violent forms of imperialist "amalgamation" of nations, leads to the break-up of multinational colonial powers. "For Communism, on the contrary, these tendencies are but two sides of a single cause—the cause of the emancipation of the oppressed peoples from the yoke of imperialism; because Communism knows that the union of nations in a single world economic system is possible only on the basis of mutual confidence and voluntary agreement, and that the road to the formation of a voluntary union of nations lies through the separation of the colonies from the 'integral' imperialist 'whole,' through the transformation of the colonies into independent states."*

Taking into account the contradictions of imperialism, Lenin and Stalin teach that Socialists belonging to ruling bourgeois nations must insist on the right to "free *secession*" for oppressed nations, whereas Socialists belonging to oppressed nations must insist on "free amalgamation."

The "critics" of Leninism claimed that these demands were "contradictory" and even paradoxical. But Lenin and Stalin teach that there is not, nor can there be, any other road to internationalism and the voluntary, i.e., the genuine amalgamation of nations. Such are the dialectics of history, the dialectics of the preparations for the victory of the proletarian revolution as the chief and decisive condition necessary for the liberation of the peoples from the yoke of capitalism.

Such is the *proletarian, international* method of liberating the oppressed nations, the method hammered out by the Party of Lenin and Stalin

---

* J. Stalin, *The Foundations of Leninism*, Moscow 1950, p. 108.

and tried and tested by the experience of the Great October Socialist Revolution.

Bourgeois nationalism as an ideology and policy, as a method of "solving" the national question, has been exposed, shattered, refuted by life itself, it has met with utter bankruptcy.

As Comrade Stalin points out, the October Revolution proved "the possibility and expediency of the *proletarian, international* method of liberating the oppressed nations as being the only correct method, having demonstrated in practice the possibility and expediency of a *fraternal union* of the workers and peasants of the most diverse nations on the principles of *voluntariness* and *internationalism*."*

Direct proof of this is provided by the development and consolidation of the multinational Soviet Socialist State and the efflorescence of the friendship among the nations of the U.S.S.R.

---

* J. Stalin, *Problems of Leninism*, Moscow 1947, p. 201.

2

THE CREATION OF THE U.S.S.R.—THE GREAT COMMONWEALTH OF SOCIALIST NATIONS

The building of our multinational socialist state opened a *new, Soviet* stage in the development of the Marxist-Leninist theory of the national question. Generalizing the experience of the building of this state and directly guiding the practical solution of the national question in the U.S.S.R., J. V. Stalin presented a profoundly Marxist-Leninist substantiation of the Soviet state's national policy and defined the ways and forms of the fraternal collaboration of the nations on the basis of the Soviet system, the ways of forming, consolidating and developing the socialist nations and their culture, which is national in form and socialist in content.

The fundamental principles of the Party's policy on the national question were formulated and scientifically substantiated by Lenin and Stalin long before the victory of the Great October Socialist Revolution.

They were proclaimed immediately after the victory of the October Revolution, in the "Declaration of Rights of the Nations in Russia" written by J. V. Stalin and published on November 16, 1917, signed by V. I. Lenin and J. V. Stalin.

The policy proclaimed in this historic document did not remain a mere declaration, as usually happens in the practice of bourgeois states. It was implemented forthwith resolutely and consistently, in the Stalin style, under the direct guidance of J. V. Stalin, then People's Commissar for the Affairs of the Nationalities.

The implementation of this policy led to an efflorescence of friendship among the nations of the U.S.S.R. such as has never been witnessed in history before; and it transformed these nations into an invincible force, into a bulwark of the freedom and independence of all the nations in the world.

On Lenin's recommendation, the Bolshevik Party entrusted the work of directly guiding the implementation of the Party's and Soviet government's national policy to J. V. Stalin, knowing that nobody was better trained than he for this work. In the first years after the October Revolution, J. V. Stalin was obliged to solve the most complicated problems connected with the Party's and Soviet government's national policy amidst the conditions of the fiercest class struggle and at the same time to direct decisive operations on the different fronts in the war against the armies of the interventionists and of the bourgeois-landlord counterrevolution.

It was only the genius of V. I. Lenin and J. V. Stalin that could ensure the implementation of the Party's correct line and policy in that complicated situation. Rebuffing the Trotskyites and nationalist deviators who were attacking J. V. Stalin, Lenin categorically declared that there was no other candidate for the post of People's Commissar for the Affairs of the Nationalities except J. V. Stalin, just as there was no other candidate for the post of People's Commissar of the Workers' and Peasants' Inspection. (J. V. Stalin had simultaneously to direct both these People's Commissariats.) "It is a gigantic task," said V. I. Lenin; it involved the solution of the most important problems of the proletarian dictatorship. Lenin pointed out that bourgeois states had been trying to solve the national problem for hundreds of years, but success had not been achieved anywhere, not even in the most democratic bourgeois republics. The Soviet system had created the possibility of solving this problem from the very outset; but in order to achieve the solution a leader was required who enjoyed the confidence of the broad masses of all the nationalities, who could be trusted to find correct, principled and just solutions of the complex problems of national interrelationships, to remove the age-long ill feeling and injustices that had been engendered by the rule of the exploiting classes. Nobody could mention a candidate other than Comrade Stalin, said Vladimir Ilyich.*

As People's Commissar for the Affairs of the Nationalities, Comrade Stalin brilliantly solved the extremely complex problems of national policy, performed gigantic theoretical and practical work in creating the national Soviet Republics and in creating and developing our multinational Soviet state. There is not a single national Soviet Republic in the creation of which Comrade Stalin did not take a decisive, leading part, and in the development of which he did not render practical assistance. It was under the direct guidance of Lenin and Stalin that the Union of Soviet Socialist Republics was created.

The masterly generalization of the experience of the revolutionary masses in building up the Soviet state made by Lenin and Stalin led to their discovery of the most suitable forms of uniting the national Soviet Republics in a single Union State—the Union of Soviet Socialist Republics (U.S.S.R.).

---

* V. I. Lenin, *Collected Works*, 4th Russ. ed., Vol. 33, pp. 281-82.

The Party and the Soviet state were then faced with a complex, gigantic, historic task, namely, to draw into the work of socialist construction those peoples in the U.S.S.R. which at the beginning of the Revolution had been in the most diverse stages of social development, from the patriarchal-nomad way of life of the outlying regions to the highly-developed industrial centres of the country. The Soviet system had first been set up in the central parts of the Union by the Russian workers; the task now was to make the tribes and peoples in our country understand this system and accept it as their own; it was necessary to build up the great commonwealth of Soviet socialist nations. Here it was necessary constructively to apply and develop the Marxist method and the Marxist science of society. The questions of self-determination, federation and autonomy were presented in a new way. Before the October Revolution, Lenin and Stalin had repeatedly opposed the application of the principle of federalism to the state structure of Russia and regarded it as a step backward toward further national segregation. The question of federation presented itself quite differently after October 1917, amidst the struggle against the bourgeois-nationalist counterrevolution and foreign intervention, when many of the peoples of our country were torn from each other, and when federation became a step forward to the amalgamation of the nations on a *Soviet socialist* basis, which facilitated friendly cooperation among the nations within the framework of a multinational Union state. J. V. Stalin showed the fundamental difference between Soviet federation based on the principle of complete equality and voluntary amalgamation and bourgeois federation, which is based on the principle of inequality, discrimination and the oppression of some nations by others.

In conformity with the principles of dialectics, J. V. Stalin teaches that Soviet federation and autonomy are not something fixed once and for all, that they permit of the most diverse forms of development. He particularly emphasizes the flexibility of Soviet autonomy and the diversity of its forms as its specific features and merits. This flexibility made it possible to deal with all the diverse national relationships, stages of historical development and class differentiations within the nations.

The correctness of the Party's policy on the national question, the flexibility and diversity of forms of Soviet autonomy and federation, enabled Soviet rule "to lay a road for itself" to the most remote outlying regions of Russia, "to rouse to political life the most backward masses of most diverse nations, to bind these masses with the centre by the most diverse threads—

a task that has not only not been carried out, but not even undertaken (they dared not undertake it!) by any other government in the world."*

Generalizing the experience of creating the R.S.F.S.R., J. V. Stalin pointed out that this type of federation was the sought for and already found form of state union that was needed to enable the Soviet Republics to develop and to preserve their existence amidst the capitalist encirclement, for "not a single Soviet Republic taken alone can regard itself as secure against economic exhaustion and military destruction at the hands of world imperialism."**

The common interests of defence and the necessity of restoring and developing the productive forces that had been destroyed by the war, J. V. Stalin pointed out, "imperatively dictate the political union of the various Soviet Republics as the only means of escaping imperialist bondage and national oppression."***

A federation of Soviet Republics, he also pointed out, is "that general form of political union which makes it possible:

---

* J. V. Stalin, *Collected Works*, Russ. ed., Vol. 4, p. 355.
** J. Stalin, *Marxism and the National and Colonial Question*, Moscow 1940, p. 81.
*** *Ibid.*

"a) to guarantee the integrity and economic development both of the individual republics and of the federation as a whole;

"b) to embrace the various social, cultural and economic conditions of the various nations and peoples, which are at different levels of development, and accordingly to apply one form of federation or another;

"c) to bring about the peaceful coexistence and fraternal collaboration of the nations and peoples which have in one form or another thrown in their lot with that of the federation."*

The experience of the R.S.F.S.R., generalized by Comrade Stalin, revealed the advantages of the Soviet federation as the state form of the Union of Soviet Republics and thereby prepared the ground for the amalgamation of all the Soviet Republics in one Union Socialist state. This state —the U.S.S.R.—was created under the direct guidance of Lenin and Stalin.

The Soviet state did not confine itself merely to establishing the political and juridical equality of nations, although this in itself was an achievement of world-historic importance, which not a single bourgeois republic, even the most democratic, can claim.

---

* J. Stalin, *Marxism and the National and Colonial Question*, Moscow 1940, p. 81.

Under the guidance of the Bolshevik Party, the Soviet state set the task of abolishing the actual inequality of nations. "The crux of the national problem in the R.S.F.S.R.," said Comrade Stalin at the Tenth Congress of the Party, "lies in the obligation to put an end to that actual backwardness (economic, political and cultural) which some of the nations have inherited from the past and to afford the backward peoples the opportunity of catching up with Central Russia politically, culturally and economically."*

This meant, among other things, that the inhabitants of the former outlying colonial regions, numbering about 25,000,000, which had not managed to go through the stage of industrial capitalism and which were several historical epochs behind Central Russia, had to "pass from primitive forms of economy to the stage of Soviet economy without passing through the stage of industrial capitalism."**

The Bolshevik Party and the Soviet state, under the leadership of J. V. Stalin, and with the assistance of the Russian working class and the Russian people, carried out this great task in an amazingly short historical period. This too reveals the immense advantages of Soviet democracy; it

---

* *Ibid.*, p. 91
** *Ibid.*, p. 92.

shows that Soviet democracy is a million times more democratic than any bourgeois democracy, which cannot and is unwilling to abolish national oppression, let alone actual national inequality. As is known, the bourgeois imperialist states are based on the oppression and exploitation of the peoples of colonies and dependent countries by a handful of dominant bourgeois nations.

J. V. Stalin showed that the source of the advantages of Soviet democracy lies in its very *economic* basis, in the nature of the socialist system of economy. Proving that the Soviet, socialist way of solving the national problem is the only correct and durable way, J. V. Stalin said:

"Whereas private property and capital inevitably disunite people, inflame national enmity and intensify national oppression, collective property and labour just as inevitably bring people closer, undermine national enmity and abolish national oppression. The existence of capitalism without national oppression is just as inconceivable as the existence of Socialism without the emancipation of oppressed nations, without national freedom."*

He showed that both the *economic* basis of the Soviet system and its *political* "superstructure"

---

* J. Stalin, *Marxism and the National and Colonial Question*, Moscow 1940, p. 79.

facilitate the voluntary amalgamation of nations, whereas in bourgeois society private property and the bourgeois state, its policy, inevitably lead to oppression, enmity and disunion among nations.

"Thus the irreconcilable contradiction between the process of economic amalgamation of the peoples and the imperialist methods of accomplishing this amalgamation was the cause of the inability, helplessness and impotence of the bourgeoisie in finding a correct approach to the solution of the national problem."* This is the basis of the inherent unsoundness, the organic instability and one of the reasons of the collapse of multinational bourgeois states.

Whereas in the bourgeois world, Comrade Stalin points out, "where capitalist democracy prevails and where the states rest on private property, the very basis of the state fosters national enmity, conflicts and struggle, here, in the realm of the Soviets, where the power is built not on capital, but on labour, where the power is built not on private property, but on collective property, where the power is built not on the exploitation of man by man, but on hostility to such exploitation, here, on the contrary, the very nature of the regime fosters a natural striving on the

---

* *Ibid.*, p. 122.

part of the toiling masses towards amalgamation in a single socialist family."*

The experience of building up the Soviet state has fully confirmed these postulates. The Soviet state succeeded in eliminating the hostility among the nations which had been fomented for centuries by tsarism and the exploiting classes which provoked mutual national massacres and pogroms.

J. V. Stalin showed that the Soviet type of state amalgamation of nations, which is based on the principle of complete equality and voluntary amalgamation, leads "to a gradual and enduring amalgamation of formerly independent nationalities in a single independent state."**

Such is the law of development of the Soviet multinational state.

*"Thus, in the Soviet system the proletariat has found the key to the solution of the national problem, has found the way to organize a durable multinational state on the basis of national equality and voluntary consent."*** J. V. Stalin appraised the creation of the U.S.S.R. as the crowning edifice on the foundations of the peaceful

---

* J. Stalin, *Marxism and the National and Colonial Question*, Moscow 1940, p. 110.
** *Ibid.*, p. 110.
*** *Ibid.*, p. 124.

and fraternal cooperation of the nations that had been laid as far back as 1917, as the creation of a mighty socialist power capable of influencing the international situation in the interests of the working people, as a new and decisive step towards the amalgamation of the working people of all countries in a single, world Socialist Republic, as the prototype of such an amalgamation.

J. V. Stalin utterly exposed the reactionary, anti-national essence of bourgeois "democracy" on the national question. All the so-called "democratic" constitutions of bourgeois states, he pointed out, are the constitutions of *dominant* nations, are *nationalist constitutions,* aimed against national minorities, against weak, small, oppressed and dependent nations.

Unlike the nationalist bourgeois constitutions, the Constitution of the U.S.S.R. is profoundly *international,* for it proceeds from the premise that all nations and races have equal rights, that differences in colour and language, cultural level, level of economic and political development, or any other differences between nations and races cannot serve as grounds for justifying inequality of nations and races. The great Stalin Constitution of the U.S.S.R. proceeds from the premise that all nations and races, irrespective of their past and present status, irrespective of whether they are weak or strong, should enjoy equal rights in all spheres of social life. The Soviet Constitution provides for legal penalties for all manifestations of propaganda of national enmity as a heinous crime against the main foundations of the Soviet, socialist system. In Soviet society there are no privileged and dominant and oppressed and unequal nations and races. Not national descent but the individual capabilities and individual labour of the citizen determine his position in Soviet society. The specific feature of the Stalin Constitution, the Constitution of Victorious Socialism, is its *consistent,* thoroughly developed *socialist democratism.*

Our people have endearingly called their Constitution the Stalin Constitution not only because J. V. Stalin is the creator of this, the greatest charter in the history of nations, in the history of mankind, but also because it was under his leadership that they achieved those splendid victories that are fixed and sealed in that Constitution. The Stalin Constitution has firmly fixed and sealed complete equality and free development for all the races and nations in the U.S.S.R. For the peoples in the capitalist countries the Stalin Constitution serves as a program of struggle; for the peoples of the U.S.S.R. it is a summation of their victories; it spiritually arms the peoples of our country, rouses their sense of national Soviet pride, mobilizes them for the struggle to achieve new victories for Communism.

All the nations and nationalities in the U.S.S.R. are today developing on a single economic basis, the basis of socialist economy, of advanced socialist industry and socialist agriculture. The formerly backward, outlying, colonial regions which had no industry, no working-class cadres and no national intelligentsia of their own, are now, thanks to the implementation of the policy of socialist industrialization, collectivization of agriculture and accelerated tempo of development, full-fledged national republics, with their own advanced industry, advanced agriculture, cadres of skilled workers, and cadres of a national intelligentsia, scientists, writers and artists. The Soviet socialist system—such is the basis of the consolidation and development of the Soviet socialist nations, which in class composition, spiritual features and social and political strivings differ fundamentally from the old bourgeois nations which arose and developed on the basis of the bourgeois order. J. V. Stalin gave a classical characterization of the old bourgeois nations and of the new socialist nations in 1929, in his splendid work *The National Question and Leninism.* In this work he made a profound generalization of all the new features the Great October Revolution and the building of Socialism had introduced in the sphere of national relationships; he disclosed the new basis of the development of nations under the Soviet system, pointed to the rise of new, Soviet, socialist nations and to the fundamental difference between them and the old, bourgeois nations. With the foresight of genius he depicted the nations' prospects of development in the period of the victory of Socialism in one country and indicated the conditions necessary for the merging of nations and national languages and cultures after the victory of Communism has been achieved all over the world.

Characterizing the nations of the U.S.S.R., Comrade Stalin said:

"These are the new, Soviet nations, which developed and took shape on the basis of the old, bourgeois nations after the overthrow of capitalism in Russia, after the elimination of the bourgeoisie and its nationalist parties, after the establishment of the Soviet system.

"The working class and its internationalist party are the force that cements these new nations and leads them. An alliance between the working class and the working peasantry within the nation for the elimination of the relics of capitalism in order that Socialism may be built triumphantly; abolition of the relics of national oppression in order that the nations and national minorities may be equal and may develop freely;

elimination of the relics of nationalism in order that friendship may be knit between the peoples and internationalism firmly established; a united front with all oppressed and unequal nations in the struggle against the policy of annexation and wars of annexation, in the struggle against imperialism—such is the spiritual, social and political complexion of these nations.

"Such nations must be qualified as socialist nations."*

These new, socialist nations arose on the ruins of the old, bourgeois nations as a result of the liquidation of capitalism, as a result of their radical transformation in the spirit of Socialism.

Comrade Stalin showed that bourgeois and socialist nations are entirely different historical types of nations, the socialist nations being more united and viable than any bourgeois nation "because they are exempt from the irreconcilable class antagonisms that corrode the bourgeois nations, and are far more representative of the whole people than any bourgeois nation."**

---

* J. Stalin, *The National Question and Leninism*, Moscow 1950, pp. 15-16.

** *Ibid.*, p. 17.

Comrade Stalin ridiculed the "theoreticians" who "overlooked the whole epoch of the formation of socialist nations in the Soviet Union, nations which arose on the ruins of the old, bourgeois nations," who refused to see the radical difference between the old, bourgeois and the new, socialist nations, refused to recognize these new, socialist nations.

The Soviet socialist nations were brought into being by the Great October Socialist Revolution. At their cradle stood the geniuses and leaders of the Revolution—V. I. Lenin and J. V. Stalin. They were led and trained in the spirit of internationalism by the great Party of Lenin and Stalin. The Soviet socialist nations developed in the direction indicated by J. V. Stalin on the basis of the Soviet, socialist system.

Comrade Stalin showed that the liquidation of the exploiting classes, the victory of Socialism, radically changed the entire social-economic and moral and political complexion of the nations in the U.S.S.R. The Soviet socialist nations consist today of a working class, a peasantry and an intelligentsia who are in friendly relations with one another and the distinctions between whom are being obliterated. The Soviet nations are socialist nations free from exploitation and class antagonisms, nations with new, Soviet, socialist moral and political features and psychological make-up.

They constitute the great commonwealth of socialist nations—the Union of Soviet Socialist Republics.

The amalgamation of the Soviet Republics did not take place without contradictions and struggle, for there were factors that hindered and counteracted this amalgamation. In his theses and report on "National Factors in Party and State Development" J. V. Stalin, at the Twelfth Congress of the R.C.P.(B.), pointed to three main factors that hindered amalgamation: growth of dominant-nation chauvinism; the actual economic and cultural inequality of the nations inherited from the past; the growth of local nationalism due to the partial revival of capitalism in the first stage of the New Economic Policy. The actual inequality of the nations could not be eliminated in a short space of time; for that many years of persevering economic and cultural development was needed. This inequality has been eliminated as a result of the implementation of the Lenin-Stalin national policy, accelerated tempo of industrialization, and the development of the industry, agriculture and culture of the formerly oppressed and backward nationalities.

The growth of industry in the U.S.S.R. as a whole was extremely rapid, but in the formerly economically backward countries it was still more rapid. Thus, in 1940, industrial output in the U.S.S.R. was 12 times as much as that in 1913. In the same period, gross industrial output in the Kazakh S.S.R. increased 22.2-fold; in the Byelorussian S.S.R. 23-fold; in the Karelo-Finnish S.S.R. nearly 50-fold; in the Kirghiz S.S.R. 160-fold, and in the Tajik S.S.R. 242-fold! This served as the basis for the growth also of the national culture of the formerly oppressed peoples; an immense cultural revolution took place in the lives of these nations.

In 1940, the number of children attending school in the U.S.S.R. as a whole was four times as high as that in the 1914-15 school year. In Kirghizia, however, the number was 44 times as high; in Uzbekistan 68 times, and in Tajikistan 660 times. From complete illiteracy and absence of culture, the formerly oppressed nations in the outlying regions have reached the pinnacles of socialist culture. More than 40 nationalities which had no written language before each acquired one under Soviet rule. The number of schools, universities, colleges, recreation centres, theatres, libraries and cinemas in these republics has increased immensely.

In 1947 there were in the Byelorussian S.S.R. 26 colleges, in the Uzbek S.S.R. 33, in the Kazakh S.S.R. 23, in the Azerbaijan S.S.R. 17, in the Armenian S.S.R. 14, in the Tajik S.S.R. 7, in the

Kirghiz and Turkmenian S.S.R. 6 each. In 1914, however, there was not a single college in the territory of any of these republics.

The Ukrainian, Byelorussian, Armenian, Azerbaijan, Kazakh, Georgian, Uzbek, Latvian, Lithuanian and Estonian S.S.R. have each their own Academy of Sciences; in other republics there are branches and bases of the Academy of Sciences of the U.S.S.R.

As a result of the gigantic work conducted by the Party and the Soviet state numerous cadres of a Soviet intelligentsia have been trained among these nationalities, numerous specialists, scientists, writers and artists.

Another factor that hindered amalgamation and the establishment of proper relations between the working class in Central Russia and the peasants in the non-Russian outlying regions was the survivals of the former mutual distrust among the formerly oppressed nations themselves and particularly their distrust, fomented by the policy pursued by tsarism and the exploiting classes, towards the Russian nation. This distrust could be overcome only by the consistent application of the Lenin-Stalin national policy; by careful consideration on the part of the Russian workers and Communists for the specifically national characteristics, ways of life, culture, interests and requirements of the working people of the formerly oppressed nations; by rendering them disinterested assistance; by prolonged joint srtuggle against their "own" and foreign oppressors and exploiters, and by cooperation in the work of building Socialism. It is precisely by applying this policy that the Russian working class and the Russian people have won the confidence and support of all the peoples of the U.S.S.R. and of the freedom-loving peoples all over the world.

Quite deservedly, J. V. Stalin has characterized the Russian people as *the most outstanding of all the nations that constitute the Soviet Union,* as the guiding force of the Soviet Union among all the peoples of our country, as the leading people, gifted with a clear mind, staunch character and revolutionary range of action.

Generalizing the experience of building up our multinational socialist state, J. V. Stalin showed that the radical change that had taken place in the economic and class structure of the U.S.S.R. as a result of the liquidation of the exploiting classes and the victory of Socialism caused radical changes also in the sphere of national relationships. When the first Constitution of the U.S.S.R. was adopted, said J. V. Stalin, the relations among the peoples of the U.S.S.R. had not yet been properly adjusted, the survivals of distrust towards the Great-Russians had not yet disappeared, the "centrifugal forces still continued to operate." These centrifugal forces had their source in private property and the exploiting classes who continued to inflame national passions and sow distrust among the peoples of our country.

"Under those conditions it was necessary to establish fraternal cooperation among the peoples on the basis of economic, political and military mutual aid by uniting them in a single, federal, multinational state."*

The Soviet government had a very clear conception of the difficulties attending this task; it had before it the unsuccessful experiments in forming multinational states in bourgeois countries. But, J. V. Stalin pointed out, "it knew that a multinational state which has arisen on the basis of Socialism is bound to stand every and any test."** And indeed, the experiment in forming a multinational socialist state was completely successful. This was a victory for the Lenin-Stalin national policy of world-historical importance. The stability of the multinational Soviet state may "well be envied by any national state in any part of the world." The Soviet state stood

---

* J. Stalin, *Problems of Leninism*, Moscow 1947, p. 546.
** *Ibid.*

the supreme test in the fires of the Great Patriotic War against the fascist invaders, a test that no other state in the world could have passed; and not only did it stand the test but emerged from it stronger and more steeled than it was before, because the mighty motive forces of Soviet society, the friendly cooperation of the workers, peasants and intelligentsia, Soviet patriotism, friendship among the peoples and their moral and political unity, had grown stronger. Generalizing the experience of the war, Comrade Stalin said that "the Soviet state system is a system of state organization in which the national problem and the problem of the collaboration of nations have found a better solution than in any other multinational state."* The Soviet socialist system has endowed the nations of the U.S.S.R. with invincible strength.

The great commonwealth of socialist nations was built up and it gained strength in the course of the uncompromising struggle the Party of Lenin and Stalin waged against nationalism of all shades and colours.

Dominant-nation chauvinism was the chief danger because it threatened to undermine the confidence of the formerly oppressed nations in the Russian proletariat, J. V. Stalin pointed out;

---

* *Speech Delivered at the Election Meeting in the Stalin Election District, Moscow, February 9, 1946*, p. 11.

it was the most dangerous enemy; it had to be crushed in order to liquidate the danger of chauvinism in general. But this did not mean, said J. V. Stalin, that a struggle had to be waged only against dominant-nation chauvinism, because the intensification of the class struggle between Socialism and capitalism activized also local nationalism; dominant-nation chauvinism and local nationalism were two sides of the same phenomenon that was inimical to the proletarian dictatorship. The deviations within the Party towards nationalism reflected the pressure of the bourgeoisie, of its policy and ideology, upon the unstable, opportunist elements that had penetrated the Party.

J. V. Stalin gave an exhaustive and profound definition of the class essence of the deviations towards dominant-nation chauvinism and local nationalism at the Twelfth, Sixeenth and Seventeenth Congresses of the Party; at the same time he indicated the way to overcome these deviations, the way to eliminate these survivals of capitalism in the minds of people as regards the national question. The deviators towards dominant-nation chauvinism came out under the flag of "internationalism," and in the name of "internationalism" they demanded that a course be taken towards the liquidation of the national Soviet Republics, towards assimilation, departure from the course of developing the culture of the different nations. Chasing after this sham "internationalism," Comrade Stalin pointed out, the deviators towards dominant-nation chauvinism fell into the net of most reactionary Kautskyan chauvinism. Kautsky, also under the flag of "internationalism," had developed the German chauvinistic idea that in the event of the victory of the proletarian revolution in Germany, the Czechs would inevitably be assimilated by the Germans.

The deviation towards local nationalism obscured the class antagonisms and the class struggle within each nation; it strove to divert the given nations from the general current of socialist development; it saw and emphasized only what could alienate the nations from each other and failed to see what drew the working people of the different nations together in their struggle for Socialism. The deviation towards local nationalism reflected the discontent of the moribund exploiting classes among the formerly oppressed nations with the regime of the proletarian dictatorship, their striving to segregate themselves in their own national bourgeois states and to establish their class rule there. The danger of this deviation lay in that it cultivated bourgeois nationalism, weakened the unity of the working people of the U.S.S.R. and played into the hands of the interventionists.

As J. V. Stalin pointed out, the two deviations towards nationalism had a common source, namely, the striving of the bourgeoisie and the bourgeois nationalist elements to adapt the proletariat's internationalist policy to the nationalist policy and class interests of the bourgeoisie. The deviations towards nationalism were particularly dangerous, because they sapped the most important source of the strength and invincibility of the nations of the U.S.S.R., namely, friendship among the nations. Nationalism, said J. V. Stalin, "is the last position held by the bourgeoisie, from which it must be dislodged in order finally to vanquish it."* Hence, the danger of nationalist survivals also becomes clear. The capitalist encirclement is constantly striving to reanimate the survivals of capitalism in people's minds, particularly in the sphere of the national question. That is why, said Comrade Stalin, we must always keep our powder dry in the struggle against all and sundry manifestations of nationalist survivals. J. V. Stalin's directions, and all his works, serve our Party and all the fraternal Communist Parties as a weapon in their struggle against the bourgeois nationalists, against the nationalist-fascist clique of Tito, Rajk, Traicho Kostov and Co., against the Right-wing Social-

---

* J. V. Stalin, *Collected Works,* Russ. ed., Vol. 4, p. 91.

ists and other agents of Anglo-American imperialism.

Generalizing the experience of building up our multinational Soviet state, Comrade Stalin showed that this experience refuted and shattered all the race theories and legends circulated by the exploiting classes to the effect that from time immemorial the world has been divided into "inferior" and "superior" races, into coloured people and whites; that the former are incapable of promoting civilization and are therefore doomed to be the objects of exploitation of the so-called "superior" races. Socialist practice in the U.S.S.R. has shown that the non-European peoples who had formerly been the objects of ruthless colonial exploitation and national oppression have also been "drawn into the channel of Soviet development, are not a bit less capable of promoting a *really* progressive culture and a *really* progressive civilization than are the European nations."*

Of exceptional importance in the struggle against nationalism and in educating the working people in the spirit of proletarian internationalism, friendship among nations and in the development and efflorescence of the national cul-

---

* J. Stalin, *Problems of Leninism*, Moscow 1947, p. 201.

tures of the peoples of the U.S.S.R. is the theory, created by J. V. Stalin, that their culture is national in form and socialist in content.

In advancing this theory, Comrade Stalin proceeded from Lenin's thesis that there are "two nations" in every bourgeois nation and two cultures in every national culture in bourgeois society.*

The "national culture" advocated by the bourgeois nationalists is the landlord, clerical and bourgeois "culture" which predominates under the conditions of capitalism. That is why Lenin described the slogan "national culture" under the conditions prevailing in bourgeois-landlord Russia as reactionary. Developing Lenin's thesis applicably to the epoch of the proletarian dictatorship, J. V. Stalin said at the Sixteenth Congress of the Party.

"What is national culture under the rule of the national bourgeoisie? It is culture that is *bourgeois* in content and national in form, having the object of doping the masses with the poison of nationalism and of strengthening the rule of the bourgeoisie.

"What is national culture under the proletarian dictatorship? It is culture that is *socialist* in

---

* V. I. Lenin, *Critical Remarks on the National Question*, Moscow 1951, pp. 17-18, 31.

content and national in form, having the object of educating the masses in the spirit of Socialism and internationalism."*

J. V. Stalin exposed the enemies of the Party who tried to identify national culture under the conditions of the Soviet system with national culture under the conditions of capitalism and on these grounds to reject the slogan of national culture in general, claiming that Lenin had done so. Comrade Stalin showed that in combating the slogan of national culture under the bourgeois order, "Lenin struck at the bourgeois *content* of national culture, but not at its national form."**

Already at the Tenth Congress of the Party, on the basis of J. V. Stalin's report, a resolution was adopted under Lenin's guidance which served as a practical program of the Party's work in developing national culture under the conditions of the proletarian dictatorship.

In his speech "On the Political Tasks of the University of the Peoples of the East" (1925), J. V. Stalin showed that there is no contradiction between the national form and the socialist content of the culture that is created under the con-

---

* J. V. Stalin, *Collected Works,* Russ. ed., Vol. 12, p. 367.
** *Ibid.*

ditions of the Soviet system. We are building proletarian socialist culture. But proletarian culture, which is socialist in content, assumes different forms and modes of expression among the different nations which have been drawn into the work of socialist construction, depending upon the different languages, ways of life, and so forth.

Comrade Stalin exposed Kautsky's chauvinistic theory according to which already in the period of the victory of Socialism in one country languages and nations must merge. Generalizing the experience of the Socialist Revolution in the U.S.S.R., Comrade Stalin pointed out that the Revolution had roused to life many previously unknown or little known new nationalities, many "forgotten" peoples and nationalities; that it endowed them with new life and new development. He predicted that the same would happen in other multinational and particularly in colonial and dependent countries; as a result of revolutionary upheavals in countries like India "scores of hitherto unknown nationalities, each with its own language and its own distinctive culture," will emerge on the scene.*

---

* J. Stalin, *Marxism and the National and Colonial Question*, Moscow 1940, p. 184.

This thesis of J. V. Stalin's exposes and upsets the various bourgeois cosmopolitan theories of the present-day Anglo-American imperialists who are pursuing the policy of forcible assimilation, the absorption of all nations and races by the "superior," "universal" Anglo-American "race."

Of exceptional theoretical and practical importance are J. V. Stalin's prescient statements concerning the future of nations, national languages and national cultures made in his work *The National Question and Leninism*.

Already in his work *Marxism and the National Question* (1913) J. V. Stalin had pointed out that a nation, like every other historical phenomenon, is subject to the law of change, has its history, its beginning and end. In developing this thesis further he proceeded from the views expressed by V. I. Lenin.

Lenin taught that the aim of Socialism is not only to abolish all segregation of nations, "not only to draw nations together, but also to merge them." But this cannot take place without a prolonged struggle against imperialism and social-chauvinism for the liberation of the oppressed nations. "Just as mankind cannot achieve the abolition of classes except by passing through the transitional period of the dictatorship of the oppressed class, so mankind cannot achieve the inevitable merging of nations except by passing through the transitional period of the complete liberation of all oppressed nations, i.e., their freedom to secede."*

After the victory of the Great October Socialist Revolution V. I. Lenin concretized these theses and pointed out that national and state differences between nations and countries "will continue to exist for a very, very long time even after the dictatorship of the proletariat has been established on a world scale."** The attempt to abolish them in the period of the proletarian dictatorship in one country he described as an "absurd dream."

Substantiating and developing these theses, J. V. Stalin points out that it would be wrong to assume that the abolition of national differences and the merging of nations, national languages and cultures will take place immediately after the defeat of world imperialism, at one stroke, by "decree from above." Attempts to bring about the merging of nations by decree from above, by means of coercion, can only play into the hands

---

* V. I. Lenin, *Collected Works*, 4th Russ. ed., Vol 22, pp. 135-36.
** V. I. Lenin, *"Left-Wing" Communism, an Infantile Disorder*, Moscow 1950, p. 127.

of the imperialists; they would be fatal to the cause of liberating the nations and of organizing their fraternal cooperation. Such a policy would be on a par with the anti-national, reactionary policy of assimilation that was pursued by the tsarist, Turkish, Persian, Prussian and Austrian assimilators, and is now being pursued by the Anglo-American imperialists who are striving to thrust upon all nations their Anglo-American "way of life," their corrupt, reactionary bourgeois "culture," in order to enslave all the nations and establish their world domination. But history shows that, being anti-national and counterrevolutionary, the assimilation policy is always, in the long run, doomed to inevitable failure.

In his work *The National Question and Leninism*, J. V. Stalin gives a forecast of genius of the probable course of "events, as regards the development of nations directly after the defeat of world imperialism."

Comrade Stalin points out that the first stage of the period of the world dictatorship of the proletariat will be the stage of the final liquidation of national oppression and of mutual national distrust, the stage of arranging and strengthening international intercourse among the nations, of the growth and efflorescence of the formerly oppressed nations and languages.

"Only in the second stage of the period of the

world dictatorship of the proletariat, as a single socialist world economy is built up in place of the capitalist world economy—only in that stage," said Comrade Stalin, "will something in the nature of a common language begin to take shape; for only in that stage will the nations feel the need to have, in addition to their own national languages, a common international language— for convenience of intercourse and for convenience of economic, cultural and political cooperation. Consequently, in this stage, national languages and a common international language will exist side by side. It is probable that, at first, not one world economic centre will be formed, common for all nations and with one common language, but several zonal economic centres for separate groups of nations, with a separate common language for each group of nations, and that only later will these centres combine into one common world socialist economic centre, with one language common to all the nations."*

This scientific prediction of genius is based on a profound analysis of the laws governing the development of society.

Comrade Stalin teaches that national distinctions and languages will begin to die out and

---

* J. Stalin, *The National Question and Leninism*, Moscow 1950, pp. 27-28.

make way for a world language common for all nations only in the third stage of the period of the world dictatorship of the proletariat—when the world socialist system of economy has become sufficiently consolidated and Socialism has become part and parcel of the life of the peoples, and when practice has convinced the nations of the superiority of a common language over national languages.

Developing these theses at the Sixteenth Congress of the Party, Comrade Stalin pointed out that the period of building Socialism in the U.S.S.R. was the period of the efflorescence of national cultures that are socialist in content and national in form. "The national cultures must be allowed to develop and unfold, to reveal all their potentialities, in order to create the conditions for merging them into one common culture with one common language in the period of the victory of Socialism all over the world. The efflorescence of cultures that are national in form and socialist in content under the proletarian dictatorship in one country *for the purpose* of merging them into one common socialist (in form and in content) culture, with one common language, when the proletariat is victorious all over the world, when Socialism has become the way of life—herein, precisely, lies the dialectics of the

Leninist presentation of the question of national culture."*

In his masterly work *Marxism in Linguistics,* J. V. Stalin exposed N. Y. Marr's vulgar theory that language is a superstructure and his formulation of language as "class language," which led to the denial that a given language is the language of the entire people, of the entire nation. J. V. Stalin proved that a language has always been a *single and common* language for all the members of the given clan, tribe, nationality or nation, for all the members of society, irrespective of their class status. He showed that the development of language is determined by the development of society, that the development of languages proceeded from the primitive, ancient languages of the clans and tribes to the languages of the nationalities, and from the latter to the languages of the nations, which are a continuation and development of the languages that were born in hoary antiquity. He also showed that there is no need for a language revolution in the period of the Socialist Revolution, as Marr and his pupils claimed, because the already evolved national languages can serve the socialist nations and their culture equally as well as they had for-

---

* J. V. Stalin, *Collected Works,* Russ. ed., Vol. 12, p. 369.

merly served the bourgeois nations and their culture. Language is the national form of a given culture. At the same time, J. V. Stalin pointed to the radical difference between the laws of development of national languages under the conditions of Socialism and those under the conditions of forms of society in which there are class antagonisms, particularly in capitalist society. He pointed out that in the epoch preceding the victory of Socialism on a world scale, when the exploiting classes are the dominant force in the world, when national and colonial oppression is still in force, when national segregation and mutual distrust among nations are fostered by state distinctions, when equality of nations has not yet been established and when the conditions for peaceful and friendly cooperation among the nations and languages do not yet exist, the development of language does not proceed by way of cooperation and the mutual enrichment of languages, but by way of assimilation, the defeat of some languages and the victory of others. It will be altogether different under the conditions of Socialism, especially after the victory of Socialism on a world scale, when world imperialism will no longer exist, when the exploiting classes will have been overthrown, when national and colonial oppression will have been abolished, when national segregation and mutual distrust among the nations will have been superseded by mutual confidence and rapprochement among nations, when equality of nations will have been established, when the policy of suppressing and assimilating languages will have been abolished and the cooperation of nations will have been established. Under these conditions, the national languages will be able freely to enrich each other in the course of cooperation. "It goes without saying," Comrade Stalin points out, "that under these conditions there can be no question of the suppression and defeat of some languages and the victory of others. Here we will have to deal not with two languages, one of which will sustain defeat and the other will emerge victorious from the struggle, but with hundreds of national languages, from among which, as a result of long economic, political and cultural cooperation among the nations, the most enriched, single zonal languages will at first emerge, and later, these zonal languages will merge into one, common international language, which, of course, will be neither German, nor Russian, nor English, but a new language, which will have absorbed all the best elements of the national and zonal languages."*

In these theses J. V. Stalin has drawn a won-

---

* J. V. Stalin, *Marxism in Linguistics*, Russ, ed., p. 54.

derfully clear prospect of the development of the socialist nations, their national languages and cultures, both in the period of the victory of Socialism in one country, namely, our country, and in the period of the victory of Socialism in other countries, and in the whole world. They are an exceptionally striking manifestation of J. V. Stalin's genius for scientific foresight; they are a splendid example of his masterly handling of materialist dialectics and reveal him as the greatest theoretician in creative Marxism. They serve as guides in all the social sciences, in philosophy, in the science of the state, in law, language, the theory of-literature, art and of culture as a whole, as well as in the practical activities of the Communist Parties in all countries in the world, especially in the sphere of national policy.

It follows from the Lenin-Stalin theory of the nation and national culture that on the national question the Communist Parties must consistently adhere to the principle of proletarian internationalism, that they must champion the right of nations to self-determination, including the right to secede from the imperialist states that oppress them and form their own, independent national states; they must champion the *proletarian, international* method of liberating the oppressed nations, train the nations in the spirit of internationalism and fraternal cooperation in the struggle against imperialism and in the building of Socialism; they must fight for the transformation of the bourgeois nations into socialist nations on the basis of the Socialist Revolution and the socialist system; they must do all in their power to promote the development of the national statehood, national economy and culture—national in form and socialist in content—of all nations, and particularly of the formerly oppressed nations, in order to enable them to enter the current of socialist development in the only way possible for them. It follows from the Lenin-Stalin theory of the nation and national culture that internationalism is engendered in culture not by belittling, impoverishing and least of all by suppressing national culture (the assimilation policy), but by developing cultures that are national in form and socialist in content. Socialist culture trains the working people in the spirit of internationalism, in the spirit of full equality and friendly cooperation among all nations and races, in the spirit of Soviet patriotism, which is not based on racial and nationalist prejudices, but on friendship among nations, on love of our Socialist Motherland; it harmoniously combines the national traditions of the peoples with the common vital interests of all the working people of the U.S.S.R. Soviet patriotism trains the people to love their own national culture and to respect the culture of other nations. In our epoch it is impossible to be an internationalist unless one is a Soviet patriot. Proletarian internationalism finds its highest historical incarnation in Soviet patriotism and friendship among the nations of the U.S.S.R.; it is uncompromisingly hostile to the anti-patriotic ideology of bourgeois cosmopolitanism and national nihilism. "National nihilism," Comrade Stalin points out, "only harms the cause of Socialism, for it plays into the hands of the bourgeois nationalists."*

The Soviet people are patriots and internationalists. They proceed from the thesis that "every nation, big or small—it makes no difference—has its own, specific qualities, specific features, peculiar to itself and not possessed by other nations. These specific qualities are the contribution each nation makes to the common treasury of world culture and augments, enriches it. In this respect all nations—big and small—are in the same position, and each nation is the equivalent of every other nation."** Comrade Stalin showed that internationalism in culture means respect for the cultural creativeness of all nations; this internationalism is engendered, fostered and developed

---
* J. V. Stalin, *Collected Works*, Russ. ed., Vol. 4, p. 91.
** *Bolshevik*, 1948, No. 7, p. 2.

on the basis of the development and efflorescence of the culture—national in form and socialist in content—of all the socialist nations and not by impoverishing national cultures and obliterating their specific national features.

It was quite natural, therefore, that the nations of the U.S.S.R., whom the Party of Lenin and Stalin has trained in the spirit of Socialism, proletarian internationalism and friendship among the nations, saved world civilization from the fascist vandals and are today at the head of the camp of Socialism and democracy, in the van of the srtuggle for lasting, democratic world peace.

The U.S.S.R. is a great commonwealth of socialist nations which are creating a new, higher, genuinely progressive, world-wide, communist culture under the leadership of the Party of Lenin and Stalin. This commonwealth grew, gained strength and vanquished all its enemies—internal and external—thanks to the wise Lenin-Stalin national policy and the ideology of friendship among nations.

Friendship among the nations of the U.S.S.R. is the expression of the internationalism of the Soviet, socialist nations, the internationalism that is embodied in the very organization of our multinational socialist state, in the organization of the Soviet social and state system, in its culture and ideology, in the self-sacrificing labours and heroic feats of the Soviet people, the Soviet patriots; it is the internationalism of nations which have been liberated from exploitation and exploiters, the internationalism of liberator nations. The nations of the U.S.S.R. are fighting in the cause, the victory of which will guarantee the liberation of all toiling humanity from the yoke of capitalism. Precisely for this reason the international proletariat and the working people of all countries support the U.S.S.R. and its policy. This is the source of the strength, the might and invincibility of the nations of our country. The nations of our country became free and invincible thanks to the Lenin and Stalin policy of friendship among the nations, to the fact that they have remained true to the ideas of proletarian internationalism. So long as this friendship exists, says Comrade Stalin, we need fear no enemies. Therefore, we must continue to *"remain true to the end to the cause of proletarian internationalism, to the cause of the fraternal alliance of the proletarians of all countries."**

* * *

The victory of the Great October Socialist Revolution involved a new presentation of the national and colonial question. Generalizing the ex-

---

* J. Stalin, *Problems of Leninism*, Moscow 1947, p. 519.

perience of the Revolution and of movements for national liberation, Lenin and Stalin further elaborated the question of the alliance of these movements with the Land of Victorious Socialism for the common struggle against imperialism. Lenin emphasized that after the Soviet Republic had been formed it was no longer possible to confine ourselves to proclaiming the drawing together of the working people of the different nations, that "it is necessary to pursue a policy that will achieve the closest alliance of all the national and colonial liberation movements with Soviet Russia, the form of this alliance to be determined by the degree of development of the communist movement among the proletariat of each country, or of the bourgeois-democratic liberation movement of the workers and peasants in backward countries among backward nationalities."* Such is the chief condition for the liberation of the oppressed nations from the yoke of imperialism.

Developing this thesis of V. I. Lenin's in the struggle against the bitterest enemies of Communism, J. V. Stalin pointed out that in our times the genuine revolutionary and internationalist is "he who without reservation, without hesitation, without conditions, is ready to defend the

---

* V. I. Lenin, *Collected Works,* 4th Russ. ed., Vol. 31, p. 124.

U.S.S.R. because the U.S.S.R. is the base of the world revolutionary movement, and it is impossible to defend, to promote this revolutionary movement unless you defend the U.S.S.R."*

J. V. Stalin teaches that the mutual cooperation and friendship of the People's Democracies and their cooperation with the U.S.S.R. are the chief conditions for the upswing and efflorescence of these People's Democracies on the socialist development front, the chief guarantee against encroachments upon their freedom and independence by imperialism. That is why, whoever, no matter in what guise, strives—as the fascist-nationalist Tito-Rajk-Traicho Kostov clique is doing —to undermine this cooperation and friendship is the worst enemy of Communism, of the working-class movement and national-liberation movement, is an agent of United States imperialism.

The victory of the Great October Socialist Revolution, the appearance of the Soviet Republic, which has abolished national and colonial oppression in the territory of a vast state and has struck a mortal blow at imperialism, inspired the oppressed nations of the East and of the whole world, created for them a mighty bulwark and shining beacon indicating the road to liberation,

---

*J. V. Stalin, *Collected Works*, Russ. ed., Vol. 10, p. 51.

united them in a common fighting front against imperialism, and actually converted this front into a part of the world socialist revolution against world imperialism.

"This means that the October Revolution has *ushered in* a new era, the era of *colonial* revolutions which are being conducted *in the oppressed countries* of the world *in alliance* with the proletariat and *under the leadership* of the proletariat....

"The era of undisturbed exploitation and oppression of the colonies and dependent countries *has passed away*.

"The era of revolutions for emancipation in the colonies and dependent countries, the era of the awakening of the *proletariat* in these countries, the era of its *hegemony* in the revolution, *has begun*."*

The October Revolution ushered in a new period in the history of the movements for national liberation and in the solution of the national and colonial problem. Characterizing the Bolshevik Party's policy in that period, J. V. Stalin points out that the chief thing here is to link the solution of the national problem with the destiny of the socialist revolution.

"The Party held that the overthrow of the

---

* J. Stalin, *Problems of Leninism*, Moscow 1947, p. 202

power of capital and the establishment of the dictatorship of the proletariat, the expulsion of the imperialist troops from the colonial and dependent countries and the securing of the right of these countries to secede and to form their own national states, the elimination of national enmity and nationalism and the strengthening of international ties between peoples, the organization of a single socialist national economy and the establishment on this basis of fraternal cooperation among peoples constituted the best solution of the national and colonial question under the given conditions.

"Such was the policy of the Party in that period."*

This period, said Comrade Stalin in 1929, "is still far from having entered into full force, for it has only just begun; but there is no doubt that it will yet have its decisive word to say."**

Twenty years have passed, and we see striking confirmation of J. V. Stalin's forecast, we see how this period is more and more entering into full force, determining the destiny of the hundreds of millions of inhabitants of the colonies and dependent countries.

---

* J. Stalin, *The National Question and Leninism*, Moscow 1950, p. 33.
** *Ibid.*

V. I. Lenin pointed out that the outcome of the world struggle between capitalism and Communism depends in the long run on the fact that the inhabitants of Russia, India and China constitute the vast majority of the population and that since the victory of the October Revolution this majority is being drawn into the struggle for its emancipation with unprecedented rapidity. With the victory of the Chinese people over imperialism and the formation of the Chinese Democratic Republic, the People's Democracies in Europe and Asia, together with the Soviet Union, account for a population of about 800,000,000—more than a third of the population of the globe!

As far back as 1925, Comrade Stalin said from the rostrum of the Fourteenth Congress of the Party that the forces of the revolutionary movement in China were immense, that they had not yet made themselves properly felt, and that they must make themselves felt in the future:

"The rulers in the East and West who do not see these forces and do not reckon with them to the degree that they deserve will suffer for this."*

---

* J. Stalin, *Political Report of the Central Committee to the Fourteenth Congress of the C.P.S.U.(B.)*, Moscow 1950, p. 48.

Truth and justice are entirely on the side of the Chinese revolution, said Comrade Stalin.

"That is why we sympathize and will continue to sympathize with the Chinese revolution in its struggle to liberate the Chinese people from the yoke of the imperialists and to unite China in a single state. Whoever does not and will not reckon with this force certainly stands to lose."*

J. V. Stalin further pointed out that the foreign imperialists who are trying to turn back the course of China's history with the aid of guns, artillery, would meet with inevitable failure, because "the laws of history are more potent than the laws of artillery."

Comrade Stalin pointed out that the Chinese revolution would not proceed along the "Kemalist" road, the road of the ordinary, restricted bourgeois revolution, that it would proceed along the road of an anti-imperialist, people's revolution and bring about the creation of an anti-imperialist people's government which would lead China along the road of socialist development.

All these forecasts of genius have been brilliantly confirmed.

With the victory of Chinese democracy the struggle for national liberation waged by the peoples of Asia, the Pacific and the whole of the co-

---
* *Ibid.*

lonial world has risen to a new and higher stage. The victory of the Chinese people greatly augments the forces and strengthens the positions of the camp of Socialism and democracy that is headed by the U.S.S.R. and is fighting for lasting democratic world peace. This victory has struck another crushing blow at the whole of the colonial system of imperialism which is experiencing a profound crisis.

The *hegemony of the proletariat* in the movements for national liberation in the colonies and dependent countries is the *new* and *decisive* factor that lends them stability, organization and invincible strength and leads to victory over imperialism. As Comrade Stalin warned, the national bourgeoisie in these countries are more and more openly entering into a compact with the foreign imperialists and betraying the national interests of their countries.

Another new factor in the movement for national liberation is that the developed capitalist countries in Western Europe which have fallen under the yoke of the United States imperialists are also being more and more drawn into it. These movements for national liberation are from the very outset developing under the *hegemony of the proletariat*, under the leadership of its Communist vanguard, and are directly merging with the struggle for *Socialism*. Evidence of this is provided by the struggle the peoples of Europe waged against the Hitler yoke during the Second World War, by the struggle they are now waging against bondage to Anglo-American imperialism, and by the establishment of the People's Democracies in Eastern and South-Eastern Europe.

The bourgeoisie in the capitalist countries of Europe are now acting as the allies of aggressive American imperialism which is preparing a new world war. That is why, as is stated in the decisions of the Information Bureau of Communist Parties, the Communist and Workers' Parties in the capitalist countries "consider it their duty to merge into one the struggle for national independence and the struggle for peace, indefatigably to expose the anti-national, treasonable character of the policy of bourgeois governments that have become direct agents of aggressive American imperialism, to unite and rally all the democratic patriotic forces of their country around the slogans calling for an end to be put to the disgraceful bondage which finds expression in servile subordination to the American monopolies, and for a return to an independent foreign and domestic policy conforming to the national interests of the peoples."*

---

* Meeting of the Information Bureau of Communist Parties, in Hungary in the latter half of November 1949, pp. 13-14.

The existence of the Soviet Union is the decisive factor that facilitates and determines the successes and victories of all the peoples' movements for national liberation in the dependent countries and colonies, because its very existence in itself puts a curb on the dark forces of reaction, inspires the oppressed peoples to fight for their liberation and facilitates this liberation.

The movements for national liberation are gaining victories because, and insofar as, they lean on the might of the U.S.S.R., enter into ever closer alliance with the U.S.S.R. and rally around it, as Lenin and Stalin taught; these movements are gaining victories because they are headed by the working class and the Communist Parties which are armed with the revolutionary Lenin-Stalin theory, strategy and tactics, and are led and inspired by great Stalin.

Stalin—the name of the genius, continuator of the great teachings and cause of Marx, Engels and Lenin, has become the symbol and fighting banner of the liberation of the peoples from the yoke of imperialism, the banner of proletarian internationalism. The great ideas of the Lenin-Stalin friendship and fraternity of the nations which are building a new world are today inspiring hundreds of millions of the common people in all parts of the world to fight for their emancipation.

The Great October Socialist Revolution and Socialism triumphed in the U.S.S.R. under the banner of proletarian internationalism, under the great banner of Marx, Engels, Lenin and Stalin. This banner has rallied around itself the great commonwealth of socialist nations of the U.S.S.R.; it is rallying around the U.S.S.R. the People's Democracies. This banner will rally around itself the whole of toiling mankind and will lead to the creation of the great world commonwealth of socialist nations.

Printed in the Union of Soviet Socialist Republics

CPSIA information can be obtained
at www.ICGtesting.com
Printed in the USA
LVHW081141020822
724960LV00004B/122